A GUIDE TO OCEAN DUNE PLANTS COMMON TO NORTH CAROLINA

Written and Illustrated by
E. Jean Wilson Kraus

Edited by
Sarah Friday

Published for
The University of North Carolina
Sea Grant College Program
by The University
of North Carolina Press

Chapel Hill
London

■

To the memory of
Dr. Kemper L. Callahan,
dedicated and
enthusiastic
teacher of biology

Illustrations by the author
Book design by Linda Noble

UNC Sea Grant College
Publication UNC-SG-87-01

This work was partially sponsored
by the Office of Sea Grant, NOAA,
U.S. Department of Commerce,
under Grant No. NA86AA-D-SG046,
the North Carolina General Assem-
bly, and the North Carolina Maritime Museum. The U.S. Government
is authorized to produce and dis-
tribute reprints for governmental
purposes notwithstanding any copy-
right that may appear hereon.

The North Carolina Maritime
Museum, Beaufort, is a division of
the North Carolina Department of
Agriculture.

**Library of Congress Cataloging-in-
Publication Data**

Kraus, E. Jean Wilson
(Elizabeth Jean Wilson)
  A guide to ocean dune plants
common to North Carolina.
  Bibliography: p.
  Includes index.
  1. Sand dune flora—North
Carolina—Identification. 2. Coastal
flora—North Carolina—
Identification. I. Friday, Sarah.
II. UNC Sea Grant College
Program. III. Title.
QK178.K73   1988 581.9756 87-40515
ISBN 0-8078-4212-5 (pbk.)

04 03 02 01 00   7 6 5 4 3

TABLE OF CONTENTS

PREFACE

The interest among schools, colleges and the public in learning about coastal ecology and biology inspired the writing of *A Guide to Ocean Dune Plants Common to North Carolina*. This book was written as a companion to *A Guide to Salt Marsh Plants Common to North Carolina* to aid in identification of the unique plants that grow on ocean dunes. Taxonomy follows the *Manual of the Vascular Flora of the Carolinas*. A background in botany is not necessary to use and enjoy this book for field or classroom study.

This book introduces the ocean dune environment and plant habitats and explains how plants survive the harsh conditions. The keys to identify common plants can be used by teachers, students, beginners in botany and visitors to the coast. Terms in the book are illustrated for easier use of keys and descriptions. Illustrations and brief descriptions aid in identification and give interesting information about each plant. Since it is impossible to include all plants that may occur on dunes, additional plants are listed that may be weedy, uncommon or may be confused with dune plant species. Most plants listed for North Carolina are typical of the mid-Atlantic coast.

The author is a botanist and educator at the North Carolina Maritime Museum in Beaufort, and also wrote *A Guide to Salt Marsh Plants Common to North Carolina*. She enjoys working in the field with people who study the coastal environment and its unique plants and animals.

Barrier islands can be described as a narrow chain of islands that parallel the eastern and southern shorelines of the United States. In North Carolina, the barrier islands from Ocracoke to Virginia are known as "The Outer Banks." Prominent features of barrier island systems include beaches, dune ridges and swales, maritime forests and salt marshes.

Barrier islands protect the mainland against the brunt of the ocean's energy. This energy is generally dissipated over the beach and dune ridges, but can cause erosion or overwash. Yet the level of defense against waves, winds, tides and storms depends upon the height and stability of the dunes. Dune and barrier island stability is influenced by geologic history and the long axis orientation of the island to the prevailing wind directions.

Geologically, barrier islands tend to be more stable if Pleistocene sediments deposited prior to the last Ice Age (2 million years ago) underlie more recent sediments. Islands that formed later tend to be more mobile and unstable.

When barrier islands are oriented with the long axis perpendicular to the dominant wind directions, they tend to be more stable with well-developed dune ridge and swale topog-raphy. An island oriented in a general east/west direction is most stable with the prevailing winds in the summer coming from the southwest and the northeast in the winter. Sustained prevailing winds can build up more sand on barrier islands than short-lived storm and hurricane winds. The large, stable dunes on relatively wide islands allow greater vegetation development and growth of a maritime forest. East/west-oriented islands such as Shackleford and Bogue Banks have high, stable dune ridges. Maritime forests are also well-developed on the stable east/west portions of Hatteras Island near Buxton and on Currituck Banks near Kill Devil Hills and Kitty Hawk.

In contrast, when the long axis of barrier islands is parallel to the dominant wind directions, dune ridge and vegetation development is poor. Less sand is transported from beaches to dunes, so the islands remain low, narrow and subject to frequent washovers. The north/south-oriented islands of Currituck Banks, Hatteras Island and Core Banks are examples.

To better understand the ocean dune environment, think about the orientation of the barrier island and the physical forces that influence dune development.

THE VALUE OF OCEAN DUNES

Barrier islands protect the mainland against strong ocean winds, tides and storms. These islands are also critical in protecting estuarine resources as nursery areas for fish and shellfish. Despite their value as protection for coastal communities and estuaries, the islands generally are unstable because of frequent overwash, erosion and sand movement.

Oceanfront dunes receive the main impact of the ocean's energy. Large dunes stable enough to withstand this impact protect the leeward sides (the sides protected from the wind) of barrier islands, especially the salt-sensitive maritime forest.

People value barrier islands and dunes for recreation and places of unique beauty. When oceanfront development results in dune destruction, natural protection against storms is diminished. If frontal dunes are destroyed, either by construction or storms, salt spray gradually kills the exposed vegetation. When sand becomes more mobile, structures are also less protected. Artificial means of stabilizing beaches and dunes, such as bulldozed dunes, sea walls and jetties, often result in greater loss of waterfront property. Wave energy would gradually tear away at dunes without normal sand replenishment from longshore currents and overwash.

Stable dune systems persist when erosion is balanced by natural sand replenishment. Vegetation is also vital in maintaining accumulated sand on dunes. Ultimately, the stability of barrier islands depends on stable dune systems.

The physical forces of the ocean determine the shape and topography of barrier islands. Waves, tides, currents, high winds and storm surges continually redistribute sand and reshape dunes. The processes of sand erosion, migration or build-up is not uniform over a barrier island, causing irregular ridge and swale topography.

Physical forces affecting dunes:

- **Storm waves, high tides and currents** may erode or wash dunes away.
- **Winds** may build up dunes or blow dune sand away.
- **Winds** can concentrate in low areas, resulting in a large hole or blowout.
- **Gentle waves** may wash sand ashore from the inner continental shelf.
- **Storm waves and tides** deposit sand in overwash fans between dunes where new dunes may begin to form.
- **Longshore currents** supply new sand to beaches that can blow onto dunes.

THE PLANT HABITAT

Plant establishment on the beach is impossible. Roots cannot take hold on constantly shifting sand or in moving salt water. But plants can take root just above the high tide line where sand accumulates.

The establishment of vegetation is important in the process of building and stabilizing dunes. When windblown sand is caught by obstacles such as plants, a dune begins to take shape around it. When accumulated sand covers dune grasses, rhizome growth through the sand aids in holding the dune in place and increases dune stabilization. Plants must tolerate and survive a variety of harsh environmental conditions for successful vegetative growth on dunes.

Dune plant habitat features:

- **Wind-carried salt spray** limits vegetative growth on frontal dunes to salt tolerant plants.
- **Salt spray** kills the exposed tips of less tolerant shrubs and trees on rear dunes causing a stunted and pruned appearance.
- **Storm waves, high waves and overwash** may uproot and wash away plants growing on frontal dunes.
- **Coarse sand** quickly drains rainwater leaving a limited supply of fresh water for plants.
- **Few soil nutrients** are available to plants since little decaying plant and animal matter accumulates on the sand.
- **Intense sunlight** reflected by the sand, in combination with constant winds, causes plants to dehydrate.
- **Extremes of hot and cold temperatures** on the exposed sand must be tolerated by plants.
- **High winds** bury plants with sand or expose plant roots to the air.
- **High winds** may break or flatten standing plants.

The establishment of vegetation benefits dune growth and stabilization. As dunes grow higher and wider, a dune line gradually forms parallel to the shoreline. With increasing stability, there is gradual transition from open dune vegetation near the ocean, to shrub thickets and maritime forests on protected dune ridges and swales across the barrier island.

Plants growing in very dry conditions such as on ocean dunes are called xerophytes. To survive in harsh habitats, dune plants have developed specialized adaptations. Look closely at plant leaves, stems, growth habit and rhizomes for clues about how each plant lives in the dune environment.

- **Waxy, leathery or fleshy leaves** resist salt damage and retain moisture (yaupon, wax myrtle, sea elder, sea rocket and seaside goldenrod).
- **Hairs on leaves** trap and retain moisture, and resist salt spray (golden aster, blanket flower and croton).
- **Inrolled leaves** minimize dehydration by reducing surface area and preventing water loss from surface pores (sea oats, running beach grass and salt meadow hay).
- **Leaves oriented in a vertical position** during the day decrease the exposed surface to the sun (pennywort).
- **Leaves flattened against the sand** withstand high winds and trap sand (sea purslane, pigweed and sea spurge).
- **Flexible stems and leaf blades** withstand high winds without breaking (sea oats, American beach grass and running beach grass).

- **Succulent stems** store water to tolerate desert-like conditions (prickly pear cactus).
- **Climbing or vine growth habits** enable plants to hug dunes or other plants for support against strong winds (morning glory, beach pea, catbrier and grape).
- **Extensive rhizome systems** (underground stems) bind loose sand and prevent plants from washing or blowing away (sea oats, American beach grass and salt meadow hay).
- **Rhizomes continue growing** if plants are buried by moving sand or if rhizomes become exposed to the air (sea oats, American beach grass).
- **Seeds, broken rhizomes and fragments of plants** may be dispersed by water on the frontal dunes (sea oats, running beach grass and sea rocket).
- **Leaf stomata** (oxygen-releasing pores) close during hot, dry days to prevent excess moisture loss through transpiration. Stomata open at night to release gases produced during photosynthesis. (Stomata on most plants open during the day and close at night.) Stomata may be sunken into the epidermis.

CONTINUED

PLANT ADAPTATIONS

- **Salt spray** provides some nutrients to plants able to absorb them through the leaves.
- **Nitrogen-fixing bacteria** occur as a symbiotic relationship in root nodules of some plants and provide this important nutrient to the plants (wax myrtle and beach pea).

Environmental factors and plant adaptations determine where plants live within a dune system. To recognize vegetation zones, think about factors that influence plant growth such as distance from the ocean, tides, waves, overwash and wind, and the influence of salt spray. Look for whether the plants are growing in well-developed soil or on windswept sand. And see if there is vegetation cover or protection behind the dunes.

The following description of the vegetation zones across a barrier island is generalized since the development of each zone depends on the width, orientation and stability of the particular barrier island. A number of plants grow in several zones, but there are recognizable habitat patterns.

- The **ocean beach** is characterized by continual wave and tidal action. Plant establishment is difficult on the beach, but sea rocket will grow near the dune line on a berm farther from the ocean where wave and tidal action is infrequent.
- The **primary or frontal dune area,** where sand accumulates above the high tide line, is habitat for a limited number of hardy plants such as sea oats, American beach grass, sea rocket and sea elder.

These plants survive battering by wind, salt spray, moving sand and storm tides.
- **Dune swales** are depressions between dune lines that offer more protection from wind and salt water. Plants found here include beach primrose, croton, seaside goldenrod, sea spurge, pennywort and occasionally wax myrtle and cottonbush.
- **Secondary or rear dunes** occurring behind frontal dune lines are subjected to wind and salt spray. Rear dunes are commonly vegetated by the same frontal dune plants, with the addition of other species such as beach pea and golden aster.
- **Shrub thickets** form behind the protection of a dune where exposure to the ocean is minimal, and fresh water is available. Wax myrtle, cottonbush and yaupon are often entangled by greenbrier and grape vines. Exposed branches are killed by salt spray, giving the shrubs a stunted and pruned appearance.
- **Maritime forests** develop toward the lee side of the island on stable dunes that are protected from the ocean. Although live oak, laurel oak, cedar, yaupon and loblolly pine are characteristic of the

CONTINUED

ZONATION

forest, deciduous hardwood trees grow in mature maritime forests such as Nags Head Woods.

- **Barrier flats or meadows** of flattened topography are formed by overwash sand. Salt meadow hay and other grasses dominate the flats.
- **Salt marshes** develop on the lee sides of barrier islands along the sounds between the high and low tide lines. Supra-tidal, salt barren, upper and lower intertidal and subtidal zones are recognized by changes in vegetation based on regular high and low tide levels. Salt marsh cord grass is the most important plant of salt marshes in terms of productivity and dominance. (The plants and zones within salt marshes are described in *A Guide to Salt Marsh Plants Common to North Carolina.*)

Barrier Island Vegetation Zonation   **Typical Plant Species**

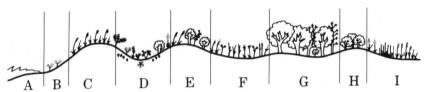

A — BEACH.

B — BERM. sea rocket, pigweed.

C — FRONTAL DUNE. sea oats, American beach grass, little bluestem, running beach grass, sea elder, seabeach orach, croton.

D — DUNE SWALE. croton, beach primrose, seaside goldenrod, sea spurge, pennywort, golden aster, beach pea, salt meadow hay, purple muhly.

E — REAR DUNES, SHRUB THICKET. sea oats, little bluestem, wax myrtle, bayberry, yaupon, cottonbush, catbrier, grapes.

F — BARRIER MEADOW (overwash sand). salt meadow hay, little bluestem, white-topped sedge, purple muhly, pennywort, croton, blue-eyed grass, spring ladies' tresses, beach primrose, marsh sedge.

G — MARITIME FOREST. live oak, laurel oak, red cedar, loblolly pine, yaupon, wax myrtle.

H — SHRUB THICKET. wax myrtle, bayberry, yaupon, cottonbush, catbrier, morning glory, marsh mallow.

I — SALT MARSH. salt marsh cord grass, black needlerush, glasswort, spike grass, seaside goldenrod.

Dune vegetation is not uniform on all North Carolina barrier islands. Some plant species only occur in the northern or the southern sections of the North Carolina coast because of a gradual climate change from north to south. The warmer climate south of Cape Hatteras is influenced by the warm Gulf Stream water flowing close to the coast. North of Cape Hatteras, where the Gulf Stream begins to flow east toward Europe, the cold Labrador (Virginia) Current cools the coastal climate.

Several North Carolina dune plants are distributed from the Cape Hatteras area north to New England. For example, bayberry *(Myrica pensylvanica)* and American beach grass *(Ammophila breviligulata)* commonly grow from Dare County to the north American beach grass rarely grows south of Pender County.

Other North Carolina dune plants grow from the Cape Hatteras area south to Florida. Sea oats *(Uniola paniculata)* replace American beach grass on dunes to the south. Pennywort *(Hydrocotyle bonariensis)*, sea rocket *(Cakile harperi)*, croton *(Croton punctatus)*, finger grass *(Chloris petraea)*, and a greenbrier *(Smilax auriculata)* commonly grow from Dare County to the south.

While studying dune plants or barrier islands, note that plant species composition varies depending on whether the barrier island is located north or south of Cape Hatteras.

PLANT DISTRIBUTION

Dare County to north
Hudsonia tomentosa—woolly
hudsonia
Myrica pensylvanica—bayberry

Dare County only
Calystegia soldanella—beach
morning glory

Dare County to south
Cakile harperi—sea rocket
Chloris petraea—finger grass
Croton punctatus—croton
Hydrocotyle bonariensis—
pennywort
Lippia nodiflora—cape weed
Smilax auriculata—greenbrier
Uniola paniculata—sea oats

Carteret County to south
Ipomoea sagittata—arrowleaf
morning glory
Ipomoea stolonifera—creeping
morning glory
Solanum gracile—nightshade
Yucca aloifolia—Spanish
bayonet

Pender County to north
Ammophila breviligulata—
American beach grass

Brunswick County to south
Baccharis glomeruliflora—
groundsel-tree

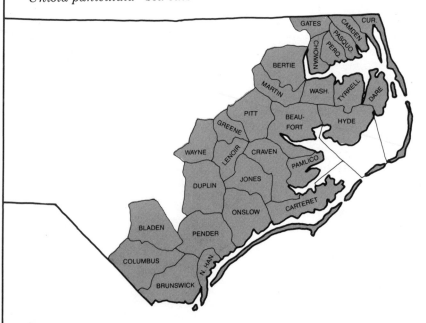

This key to common dune plants is intended for teachers, students, beginners in botany and visitors to the coast. A background in botany is not necessary to use the guide. Terms used throughout the key, such as leaf shapes and leaf margins, that may be unfamiliar are illustrated.

To use the key, first decide whether the plant in question is a tree, shrub, vine, herb or grass. A general description of each plant form is given on the following pages: tree—page 23, shrub—page 27, vine—page 33, herb—page 41, grass—page 55.

After choosing a plant form, turn the page to the simple line key. Beginning with the main heading at each level, choose one of two descriptions that fit the plant best. Continue to work through the choices until a plant is named. When a name is reached, turn to the page with the corresponding illustration and description to determine if the identification seems correct. If it is not correct, then try again.

It is possible to have a plant that is not included in the key, since only the most common plants are given. Similar plant species are listed with the descriptions of those illustrated.

Check the list of additional plant species that may also occur on dunes, but are roadside weeds or are uncommon. If you wish to study the plants further, use the *Manual of the Vascular Flora of the Carolinas* by Radford, Ahles and Bell.

ILLUSTRATION OF TERMS

LEAF ARRANGEMENTS

opposite

alternate

basal rosette

LEAF MARGINS

entire

dentate

serrate

rounded

spiny

lobed

toothed

wavy

dissected

rolled under

inrolled

LEAF TYPES

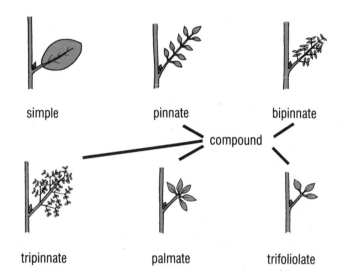

simple

pinnate

bipinnate

compound

tripinnate

palmate

trifoliolate

STEM AND LEAF STRUCTURAL TYPES

rhizome

cladode-cactus

tendril

spines

scale leaves

bracts
(leaves below flowers)

ILLUSTRATION OF TERMS

LEAF HAIR TYPES

| hirsute | star-shaped | glandular | spines and glochids |

LEAF SHAPES

| linear | lanceolate | oblanceolate | elliptic |

| ovate | obovate | triangular-ovate |

arrowhead-shaped   heart-shaped   lobed basally   round

FLOWER ARRANGEMENTS

spike

raceme

panicle

cyme

corymb

umbel

head

ILLUSTRATION OF TERMS

FLOWER TYPES

radial
(five or six petals)

cross-shaped
(four petals)

bell-shaped

trumpet-shaped

tubular

two-lipped (mints)

keeled (pea-like)

catkin (cone-like)

orchid-shaped

head

ray flower

disc flower

SPIKELETS

running beach grass (ovoid)

sea oats (flattened)

bluestem (awns)

marsh sedge
(overlapping scales, ovoid)

sandspur (spiny burs)

white-topped sedge
(bracts)

FRUIT TYPES

DRY UNSPLITTING

nutlet (sedges)

nutlet,
(achene) with bristles
(aster family)

grain (grasses)

nut (acorn) oaks

nutlet

DRY SPLITTING

capsule

capsule, silicle
(mustard family)

legume
(bean family)

cylindric capsule

FLESHY

berry
(or drupe)

berry enclosed by papery sheath

aggregate berry

TREE

- woody
- branches from a single trunk
- may be evergreen or deciduous
- a forest canopy plant

OCEAN DUNE PLANTS

TREES

Leaves elliptic to obovate, leathery; fruits are acorns—LIVE OAK *Quercus virginiana* (see page 25)

Leaves scale-like, small, overlapping; fruits are bluish berry-like cones—RED CEDAR *Juniperus virginiana* (see page 25)

T R E E

LIVE OAK
Quercus virginiana

- Oak family: Fagaceae
- Bark dark brown, ridged, branches wide-spreading, trees stunted where exposed to salt spray
- Leaves: evergreen, leathery, alternate, elliptic-obovate, margins not rolled under
- Flowers: clustered male catkins, separate female spikes, April
- Fruits: clustered acorns, Sept.–Nov.
- Habitats: dune swales, shrub thickets, maritime forests
- Wood historically used in boat-building
- Laurel oak, *Quercus laurifolia:* similar tree in maritime forests, bark smooth, trunk straight, leaves not rolled under, acorns single

RED CEDAR
Juniperus virginiana

- Juniper family: Cupressaceae
- Bark reddish-brown, shreddy
- Leaves: evergreen, blunt overlapping scales, sharp when young
- Flowers: small male and female cones, Jan.–March
- Fruits: bluish berry-like cone, Oct.–Nov.
- Habitats: dune swales, shrub thickets, maritime forests, disturbed sites
- Wood used in construction and furniture, fragrance repels insects, berries flavor gin
- Difficult to distinguish from Southern red cedar, *Juniperus silicicola,* with smaller cones

SHRUB

- woody
- branches from the base from several main stems, not usually from a single trunk
- stems persist through winter
- a forest subcanopy plant

OCEAN DUNE PLANTS

SHRUBS

Leaves elliptic, ovate, obovate, or oblanceolate, "typical" leaf structures

Leaves not as described, not "typical" leaf structures

Leaves aromatic when crushed, yellow glands on leaf surface—WAX MYRTLE *Myrica cerifera* (see page 29)

True leaves usually absent, stems are leaf-like, succulent, and green, spiny; yellow flowers are many-petaled; fruit a large berry—PRICKLY PEAR CACTUS *Opuntia drummondii* (see page 31)

Leaves not aromatic when crushed, yellow glands absent

Leaves ovate to elliptic, evergreen; flowers not in heads; fruits are red berries—YAUPON *Ilex vomitoria* (see page 29)

True leaves present, large, sharp-pointed or small, scale-like

Leaves elliptic, obovate, or oblanceolate, not evergreen; flowers in heads; fruits are tiny nutlets

Large shrub; leaves large, sharp-pointed, thick, and leathery; white bell-shaped flowers; elongate purple berry—SPANISH BAYONET, YUCCA *Yucca aloifolia* (see page 31)

Leaves gray-green; flowering heads in clusters; nutlets crowned with cottony hairs; often grows between dunes—COTTONBUSH, GROUNDSEL-TREE *Baccharis halimifolia* (see page 30)

Leaves dark green; flowering heads in racemes, encased by fleshy bracts; nutlets without cottony hairs; often grows on frontal dunes—SEA ELDER *Iva imbricata* (see page 30)

Low-growing shrub; leaves small, scale-like; tiny yellow flowers; small capsules—WOOLLY HUDSONIA *Hudsonia tomentosa* (see page 32)

S H R U B

WAX MYRTLE
Myrica cerifera

- Bayberry family: Myricaceae
- Leaves: evergreen, yellow resinous glands on both surfaces, aromatic, alternate, elliptic-oblanceolate, margins toothed
- Flowers: catkins, April
- Fruit: berry-like, waxy, less than 3.5 mm diameter, Aug.–Oct.
- Habitats: dune swales, shrub thickets, maritime forests
- Wax from berries was used in bayberry candles during colonial times. Boughs placed upon fish carts repelled flies. Leaves repel fleas.
- Bayberry, *Myrica pensylvanica:* leaves are glandular on lower surfaces only, and fruit diameter is more than 3.5 mm

YAUPON
Ilex vomitoria

- Holly family: Aquifoliaceae
- Leaves: evergreen and waxy, alternate, ovate-elliptic, margins with rounded teeth
- Flowers: small white, four petals, male and female flowers on separate plants, March–May
- Fruits: red berries (drupes), Oct.–Dec.
- Habitats: dune swales, shrub thickets, maritime forests
- Tea was a traditional coastal beverage in colonial days, and contains caffeine. Indians added berries for a stronger tea, tho "black drink," used as a purgative during religious ceremonies.

S H R U B

GROUNDSEL-TREE, COTTONBUSH
Baccharis halimifolia

- Aster family: Asteraceae
- Leaves: gray-green, alternate, elliptic-obovate, margins toothed
- Flowers: cream-colored, heads in loose clusters, male and female flowers on separate plants
- Fruits: nutlets crowned with cottony hairs, Sept.–Oct.
- Habitats: dune swales, shrub thickets, salt marsh edges
- Groundsel-tree, *Baccharis glomeruliflora:* heads of flowers in tight clusters, dune swales

SEA ELDER
Iva imbricata

- Aster family: Asteraceae
- Leaves: fleshy, alternate, elliptic-oblanceolate, margins toothed or entire
- Flowers: cream-colored, heads in racemes, encased by fleshy bracts
- Fruits: yellowish-brown nutlets, sticky, Aug.–Nov.
- Habitats: dunes, upper beach
- Marsh elder, *Iva frutescens:* leaves opposite, grows along salt marshes

PRICKLY PEAR CACTUS
Opuntia drummondii

* Cactus family: Cactaceae
* Shrub is low-growing
* Stems: succulent, green, photosynthetic, spiny
* Leaves: very small, soon deciduous, rarely seen
* Spines: two to four long spines per leaf axil, numerous hair-like spines called glochids
* Flowers: yellow, many petals
* Fruits: magenta berry, glochids present, Aug.–Oct.
* Habitats: dunes, sandy openings
* Edible: fruit pulp cooked or eaten raw
* May intergrade with *Opuntia compressa*, zero to one spine per leaf axil. Spiny berry purple to reddish brown

SPANISH BAYONET, YUCCA
Yucca aloifolia

* Lily family: Liliaceae
* Leaves: evergreen, thick and leathery, alternate, linear-lanceolate, margins serrate, sharp-pointed
* Flowers: white, bell-shaped, fleshy, June–July
* Fruits: elongate, leathery, purple berry to 9 cm long, Oct.–Dec.
* Habitats: dunes, maritime forests, salt marsh edges
* Edible: fleshy petals raw in salads or fried, ripe fruit pulp baked
* *Yucca gloriosa:* leaf margins entire

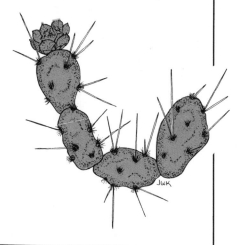

S H R U B

WOOLLY HUDSONIA
Hudsonia tomentosa

- Rockrose family: Cistaceae
- Shrub is low-growing
- Leaves: evergreen, scale-like, hairy
- Flowers: tiny, five yellow petals, May–June
- Fruits: capsule, Aug.–Sept.
- Habitat: dunes, rare

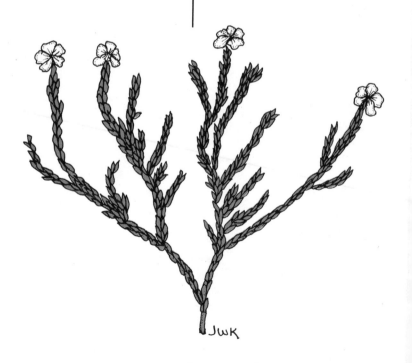

JwK

VINE

- woody or herbaceous
- perennial
- evergreen or deciduous
- trails along ground or climbs with tendrils on other plants

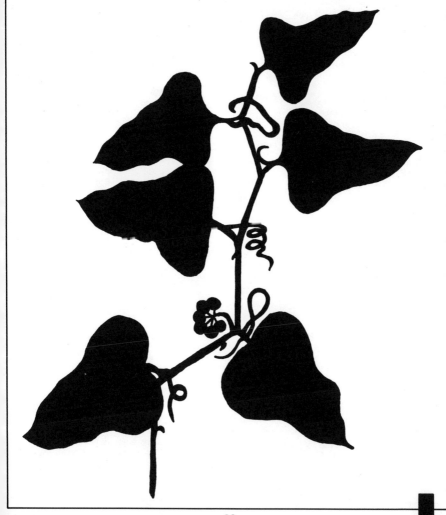

OCEAN DUNE PLANTS

V I N E

VINES

Stems usually spiny

Stems never spiny

Leaves compound, three to five leaflets, not leathery; stems with spines and glandular hairs; fruit an aggregate berry (blackberry); plant trails on ground—DEW-BERRY *Rubus trivialis* (see page 35)

Leaves arrowhead-shaped; pink, trumpet-shaped flowers—ARROWLEAF MORNING GLORY *Ipomoea sagittata* (see page 36)

Leaves not arrowhead-shaped; flowers not trumpet-shaped

Leaves simple, leathery, stems may be spiny; berries in umbels; plant may form dense thickets

Leaves simple, widely ovate

Stems usually spiny; leaves ovate to lanceolate, often with a pair of pronounced basal lobes, may be mottled color, margins often spiny; bluish-black berries—GREEN-BRIER, CATBRIER *Smilax bona-nox* (see page 35)

Leaves lobed, hairy; purple berries to 1.2 cm diameter—FOX GRAPE, SUMMER GRAPE *Vitis aestivalis* (see page 37)

Leaves not lobed, smooth—not hairy; purple berries to 2 cm diameter—MUSCADINE GRAPE *Vitis rotundifolia* (see page 37)

Stems often spineless; leaves lanceolate to oblanceolate, may have slight basal lobes, margins spineless; black berries—GREENBRIER, CATBRIER *Smilax auriculata* (see page 36)

Leaves compound, leaflets three or more, not widely ovate

Leaflets—five or more

Leaflets—three

Leaves usually shiny, often lobed; flower not showy, greenish-white; white berries—POISON IVY *Rhus radicans* (see page 38)

Leaflets—five, palmately compound; many tendrils with adhesive disks—VIRGINIA CREEPER *Parthenocissus quinquefolia* (see page 39)

Leaves not shiny, not usually lobed; flowers pea-like, keeled, pink; bean-like legumes—BEACH PEA *Strophostyles helvola* (see page 38)

Leaflets usually more than five; bi- or tri-pinnately compound; few tendrils—PEPPERVINE *Ampelopsis arborea* (see page 39)

V I N E

DEWBERRY
Rubus trivialis

- Rose family: Rosaceae
- Stems: covered with glandular hairs, spiny, trail on ground
- Leaves: palmately compound, three to five leaflets, ovate-lanceolate, margins toothed, red in winter
- Flowers: white, five petals, numerous stamens, March–April
- Fruits: compound black berry, juicy, April–May
- Habitats: dunes, disturbed areas
- Edible: "blackberries" good raw or cooked

CATBRIER, GREENBRIER
Smilax bona-nox

- Lily family: Liliaceae
- Stems: woody, low-climbing, green, spiny
- Leaves: evergreen, leathery, ovate-lanceolate, often with basal lobes, mottled color, spiny margins
- Flowers: tiny green, three petals, in umbels, April–May
- Fruits: bluish-black berries, Sept.–Nov.
- Habitats: dunes, shrub thickets, maritime forests, salt marsh edges
- Edible: young shoots eaten in salads or cooked vegetables

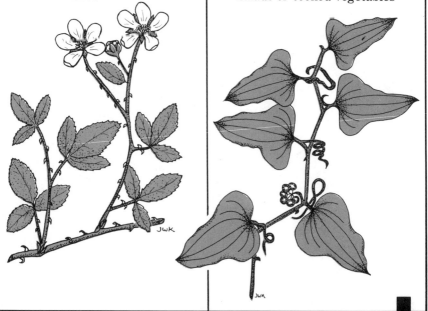

OCEAN DUNE PLANTS

CATBRIER, GREENBRIER
Smilax auriculata

- Lily family: Liliaceae
- Stems: woody, forms low thickets, green, usually spineless
- Leaves: evergreen, lanceolate-oblanceolate, may have basal lobes
- Flowers: tiny green, three petals, in umbels, May–July
- Fruits: black berry, Oct.–Nov.
- Habitats: dunes, shrub thickets, maritime forests
- Edible: young shoots eaten in salads or cooked vegetables

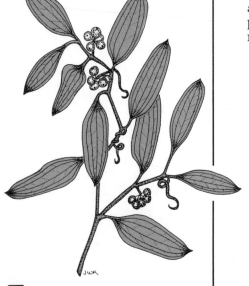

ARROWLEAF MORNING GLORY
Ipomoea sagittata

- Morning glory family: Convolvulaceae
- Stems: herbaceous
- Leaves: arrowhead-shaped
- Flowers: pink, trumpet-shaped
- Fruits: globose capsule, July–Sept.
- Habitats: dunes, salt marsh edges
- Creeping morning glory, *Ipomoea stolonifera:* flowers white, leaves violin-shaped, infrequent
- Beach morning glory, *Calystegia soldanella:* flowers rose purple, with two leafy bracts, rare

FOX GRAPE, SUMMER GRAPE
Vitis aestivalis

- Grape family: Vitaceae
- Stems: woody with tendrils, high-climbing
- Leaves: widely ovate, lobed, hairy, margins toothed
- Flowers: small yellow-green, five petals, May–June
- Fruits: dark purple berries to 1.2 cm diameter, Sept.–Oct.
- Habitats: dunes, shrub thickets, maritime forests
- Edible: grapes good raw or cooked

MUSCADINE GRAPE
Vitis rotundifolia

- Grape family: Vitaceae
- Stems: woody with tendrils, high-climbing
- Leaves: widely ovate, smooth, margins toothed
- Flowers: small yellow-green, five petals, nectar glands, May–June
- Fruits: dark purple berries to 2 cm diameter, Aug.–Oct.
- Habitats: dunes, shrub thickets, maritime forests
- Edible: grapes good raw or cooked, young leaves wrap baked food
- Horticultural varieties of muscadine are cultivated for fruit and wine-making. "Scuppernong" is a natural sport of muscadine with white grapes.

OCEAN DUNE PLANTS

POISON IVY
Rhus radicans

- Sumac family: Anacardiaceae
- Stems: woody or herbaceous, high-climbing or trailing
- Leaves: compound, three leaflets, elliptic-ovate, lobed
- Flowers: greenish-white, five petals, April–May
- Fruits: white berry, smooth or hairy, Aug.–Oct.
- Habitats: dunes, shrub thickets, disturbed areas
- A contact poison that produces a rash!

BEACH PEA
Strophostyles helvola

- Bean family: Fabaceae
- Stems: herbaceous
- Leaves: compound, three leaflets, ovate
- Flowers: pea-like, keeled, lavender, June–Sept.
- Fruits: legume, covered with fine hairs, Aug.-Oct.
- Habitat: dunes
- Edible: beans and peas can be cooked as vegetables

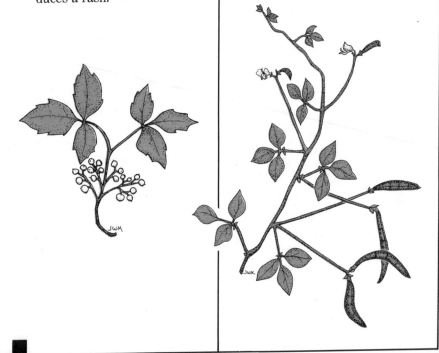

VIRGINIA CREEPER
Parthenocissus quinquefolia

- Grape family: Vitaceae
- Stems: woody, many tendrils with adhesive disks, high-climbing
- Leaves: palmately compound, leaflets elliptic-obovate, margins toothed
- Flowers: tiny yellow-green, five petals
- Fruits: dark blue or black berries (drupes), July–Aug.
- Habitats: dunes, shrub thickets, openings

PEPPERVINE
Ampelopsis arborea

- Grape family: Vitaceae
- Stems: woody, few tendrils
- Leaves: bi- and tripinnately compound, leaflets ovate, margins toothed
- Flowers: tiny yellow-green, five petals, June–Aug.
- Fruits: blue or black berries (drupes), Aug.–Oct.
- Habitats: dunes, shrub thickets, openings
- Fruits have a peppery taste

HERB

- herbaceous; lacks a persistent woody stem; dies back in winter
- may be perennial; overwinters as rhizomes or bulbs
- may be annual; entire plant dies after one growing season; propagates only by seed
- may be biennial; plant lives through two growing seasons

OCEAN DUNE PLANTS

Flowers blue, enclosed by leafy bracts; few flowers per plant—BLUE-EYED GRASS *Sisyrinchium mucronatum* var. *atlanticum* (see page 44)

Flowers white to yellowish, small orchids spiraled in dense-flowered spike— SPRING LADIES' TRESSES *Spiranthes vernalis* (see page 44)

Flower petals and sepals in threes or sixes; leaves linear-lanceolate, grass-like, parallel veins

Heads white, lavender, small; leaves linear-oblanceolate, "delicate-looking" plant— HORSEWEED *Erigeron canadensis* var. *pusillus* (see page 45)

HERBS

Multi-flowered heads appear as one flower, daisy or dandelion-like; nutlets crowned with bristles (in Aster family)

Heads yellow, orange or r

Flower petals and sepals in fours or fives; leaves not linear or grass-like, veins netted

Flowers not in heads; fruits not nutlets with bristles (not in Aster family)

Flowers showy, colorful conspicuous

Flowers small, greenish, inconspicuous

Leaves alternate, ovate-lanceolate, star-shaped hai visible with a hand lens; shrub-like—CROTON *Crot punctatus* (see page 49)

Fruit a tiny nutlet; leaves fleshy or succulent

Fruit a three-lobed capsule; leaves not fleshy

Leaves opposite, elliptic-lanceolate, not hairy; stem radiate from a central poin grows flattened on ground DUNE SPURGE *Euphorl polygonifolia* (see page 49)

Stems upright; leaves entire or toothed

Stems trailing on ground, low-growing; leaves entire with small notch at tip—PIGWEED *Amaranthus pumilus* (see page 47)

Leaves triangular-ovate, mealy and fleshy, margins toothed, tinged with purple—SEABEACH ORACH *Atriplex patula* (see page 48)

Leaves linear, succulent, margins entire, whitish-green—SEA BLITE *Suaeda linearis* (see page 48)

Stems four-sided, creepin upright; leaves may be fle

Stems hairy, upright; flowers yellowish with purple spots, two-lipped; lavender leafy bracts below flowers; odor of mint—HORSEMINT *Monarda punctata* (see page 53)

Stems not hairy, upright or flattened on ground; tiny lavender flowers in leafy button-like heads—CAPE WEED *Lippia nodiflora* (se page 53)

H E R B

eads greater than 2 cm
ide, daisy-like; orange, red
yellow color combinations—
RE-WHEEL, INDIAN
LANKET *Gaillardia*
lchella (see page 45)

Heads dandelion-like (all ray
flowers); stems very leafy;
leaves dissected, lettuce-like—
WILD LETTUCE *Lactuca
canadensis* (see page 46)

Stems and leaves hairy;
yellow heads 7 to 12 mm wide
in loose corymbs; flower
bracts with glandular hairs—
GOLDEN ASTER, CAM-
PHOR WEED *Heterotheca
subaxillaris* (see page 46)

Heads less than 1.5 cm wide,
daisy or dandelion-like; yellow
or orange-yellow

Heads daisy-like (both disc
and ray flowers); leaves fleshy
or hairy, not dissected

Stems and leaves fleshy;
yellow heads 2 to 4 mm wide,
numerous in raceme-like
panicles; no glandular hairs—
SEASIDE GOLDENROD
Solidago sempervirens (see
page 47)

Flowers yellow or tinged with
pink

Stems low or flat on ground;
leaves elliptic-oblanceolate;
flowers yellow tinged with
pink, four petals; capsules
cylindrical; entire plant
covered with silky hairs—
SEASIDE EVENING
PRIMROSE *Oenothera
humifusa* (see page 50)

Stems upright; leaves ovate-
elliptic; flowers yellow, five
petals, bell-shaped; yellow-
orange berry (tomato-like)
enclosed by papery sheath—
GROUND CHERRY, JAPA-
NESE LANTERN *Physalis
viscosa* ssp. *maritima* (see
page 50)

Flowers white, pink or
lavender

Leaves not roundish, typical
petiole attached at leaf base;
flowers not in umbels

eaves roundish, with petiole
tached in leaf center, mar-
ins with rounded teeth;
owers small, white, in umbels
-PENNYWORT *Hydro-
otyle bonariensis* (see
age 51)

Leaves opposite on stem;
flowers pink or lavender, five
petals or sepals

Leaves alternate on stem;
flowers white to pink, four
petals

ems not four-sided, creep-
g; leaves thick and suc-
lent; five pink petal-like
pals—SEA PURSLANE
esuvium portulacastrum
ee page 52)

Leaves thick and fleshy,
elliptic-lanceolate, margins
toothed; flowers white to
pink; capsule larger than 2 cm
long, rocket-shaped, two-
jointed—SEA ROCKET, SEA
KALE *Cakile harperi* (see
page 51)

Leaves not thick and fleshy,
lanceolate, margins toothed or
dissected; flowers white; capsules heart-shaped less than
.5 cm long—POOR MAN'S
PEPPER *Lepidium
virginicum* (see page 52)

OCEAN DUNE PLANTS

H E R B

BLUE-EYED GRASS
Sisyrinchium mucronatum var. *atlanticum*

- Iris family: Iridaceae
- Perennial
- Leaves: linear, grass-like
- Flowers: blue with six similar petals and sepals, enclosed by leafy bracts, March–June
- Fruits: small capsule, June–Aug.
- Habitat: dune swales, weed in disturbed areas

SPRING LADIES' TRESSES
Spiranthes vernalis

- Orchid family: Orchidaceae
- Perennial, stems hairy
- Leaves: basal and along stem, linear-lanceolate
- Flowers: white to yellowish, small orchids, flower parts in threes, spiraled in a dense spike
- Fruits: capsule, March–July
- Habitats: dune swales, wet meadows, marshes, infrequent

H E R B

HORSEWEED
Erigeron canadensis var.
pusillus

- Aster family: Asteraceae
- Annual
- Leaves: linear-oblanceolate,
  margins entire to toothed
- Flowers: small heads, white to
  lavender rays
- Fruits: nutlets crowned with
  bristles, July–frost
- Habitats: dunes, weed in
  disturbed areas

FIRE-WHEEL, INDIAN BLANKET
Gaillardia pulchella

- Aster family: Asteraceae
- Perennial, blooms all summer
  and fall
- Leaves: lanceolate-oblanceolate, margins lobed or toothed
- Flowers: heads large daisy-
  like, red-orange or yellow
- Fruits: nutlet crowned with
  bristles, April–frost
- Habitats: dunes, roadsides,
  often cultivated

OCEAN DUNE PLANTS

H E R B

WILD LETTUCE
Lactuca canadensis

- Aster family: Asteraceae
- Biennial, stems leafy
- Leaves: lanceolate-
  oblanceolate, margins toothed,
  dissected
- Flowers: orange-yellow heads
- Fruits: nutlets crowned with
  bristles, June–frost
- Habitats: dunes, weed in
  disturbed areas
- Edible: young leaves eaten in
  salads, related to cultivated
  lettuce
- Several species of *Lactuca*
  grow in disturbed areas
- Sow thistle, *Sonchus asper:*
  spiny leaves

GOLDEN ASTER,
CAMPHOR WEED
Heterotheca subaxillaris

- Aster family: Asteraceae
- Annual or perennial, taproot,
  stems hairy
- Leaves: elliptic-ovate, margins
  toothed, hairy
- Flowers: yellow heads in
  loose corymbs, bracts
  glandular
- Fruits: nutlets crowned with
  bristles, July–Oct.
- Habitats: dunes, weed in
  disturbed areas

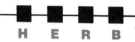

SEASIDE GOLDENROD
Solidago sempervirens

- Aster family: Asteraceae
- Perennial
- Leaves: elliptic-lanceolate, margins toothed, fleshy
- Flowers: yellow heads in panicles
- Fruits: nutlets crowned with bristles, Aug.–Nov.
- Habitats: dunes, salt marsh edges
- An herbal tea is made from leaves and flowers, similar to chamomile tea

PIGWEED
Amaranthus pumilus

- Amaranth family: Amaranthaceae
- Annual, stems trailing, low-growing
- Leaves: alternate, ovate-obovate, fleshy, slight notch at tip
- Flowers: male and female flowers on same plant, inconspicuous in leaf axils
- Fruits: tiny bladder-like nutlet, June–frost
- Habitats: upper beach and dunes, rare
- Dune amaranth, *Iresine rhizomatosa:* tall erect stems, flowers in panicles, dune swales, rare

OCEAN DUNE PLANTS

SEABEACH ORACH
Atriplex patula

- Goosefoot family: Chenopodiaceae
- Annual
- Leaves: fleshy and mealy, triangular-ovate, margins toothed, tinged with purple
- Flowers: green, inconspicuous
- Fruits: nutlet-like, July–frost
- Habitats: dunes, salt marsh edges
- Edible: leaves are good as cooked greens
- *Atriplex arenaria:* leaves are ovate-elliptic, silvery, grows only on dunes

SEA BLITE
Suaeda linearis

- Goosefoot family: Chenopodiaceae
- Annual
- Leaves: fleshy, alternate, linear, whitish-green
- Flowers: green, inconspicuous in leaf spikes
- Fruits: nutlet-like, Aug.–frost
- Habitats: dune swales, salt marshes
- Edible: leaves eaten raw in salads

H E R B

CROTON
Croton punctatus

- Poinsettia family: Euphorbiaceae
- Annual or perennial
- Leaves: alternate, ovate-lanceolate, star-shaped hairs visible with a hand lens
- Flowers: separate male and female flowers, inconspicuous
- Fruits: three-lobed capsule, May–Nov.
- Habitat: dunes

DUNE SPURGE
Euphorbia polygonifolia

- Poinsettia family: Euphorbiaceae
- Annual or perennial, stems radiate from a single root, flattened on the ground
- Leaves: small, opposite, elliptic-lanceolate
- Flowers: separate male and female flowers in clusters resembling single flowers, nectar gland, inconspicuous
- Fruits: tiny three-lobed capsules, May–Oct.
- Habitat: dunes
- Difficult to distinguish from *Euphorbia ammannioides:* smaller capsules

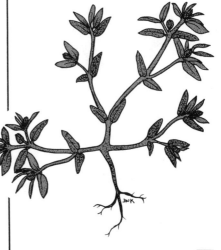

OCEAN DUNE PLANTS

H E R B

SEASIDE EVENING PRIMROSE
Oenothera humifusa

- Primrose family: Onagraceae
- Perennial, stems often flat-tened on ground, hairy
- Leaves: alternate, elliptic-oblanceolate, hairy, margins wavy
- Flowers: four petals, yellow tinged with pink
- Fruits: capsules, hairy, cylin-dric, May–Oct.
- Habitat: dunes
- Hybridizes with *Oenothera laciniata:* lobed leaves, weedy

GROUND CHERRY, JAPANESE LANTERN
Physalis viscosa ssp. *maritima*

- Tomato family: Solanaceae
- Perennial, star-shaped hairs visible with a hand lens
- Leaves: alternate, ovate-elliptic, hairy
- Flowers: yellow, five petals, bell-shaped
- Fruits: yellow-orange berry enclosed by papery sheath "lantern," May–Sept.
- Habitats: dunes, weed in disturbed areas
- Edible: berries eaten raw or cooked when fully ripe and orange; leaves and unripe fruits are poisonous
- Nightshade, *Solanum gracile:* white flowers, black berry, no papery sheath, very poisonous

PENNYWORT
Hydrocotyle bonariensis

- Carrot family: Apiaceae
- Perennial with white rhizomes (underground stems)
- Leaves: roundish, petiole attached in leaf center, margins with rounded teeth
- Flowers: small, white, five petals, in compound umbels
- Fruits: nutlet-like, similar to dill seeds, April–Sept.
- Habitats: dune swales, salt marsh edges, openings
- Stems taste similar to parsley
- Marsh pennywort, *Hydrocotyle umbellata:* simple umbels

SEA ROCKET, SEA KALE
Cakile harperi

- Mustard family: Brassicaceae
- Annual or perennial
- Leaves: fleshy, elliptic-lanceolate, margins toothed
- Flowers: tiny, pink to white, four petals
- Fruits: rocket-shaped capsule
- Habitats: upper beach, dunes
- Edible: young leaves eaten raw in salads or as cooked greens
- *Cakile edentula:* capsule is notched at top

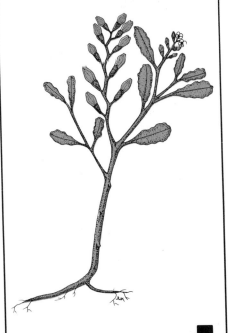

OCEAN DUNE PLANTS

H   E   R   B

SEA PURSLANE
Sesuvium portulacastrum

- Purslane family: Aizoaceae
- Perennial, creeping stems
- Leaves: opposite, oblance-olate, fleshy
- Flowers: no petals, five pink sepals
- Fruits: capsules, May–frost
- Habitats: upper beach, dunes
- *Sesuvium maritimum:* annual, some upright stems, leaves linear, stemless flowers and fruits

POOR MAN'S PEPPER
Lepidium virginicum

- Mustard family: Brassicaceae
- Annuals, basal rosette absent at flowering
- Leaves: lanceolate, margins toothed or dissected
- Flowers: small, white, four petals
- Fruits: heart-shaped capsule, April–June
- Habitats: dunes, weed in disturbed areas
- Edible: capsules used as pepper substitute

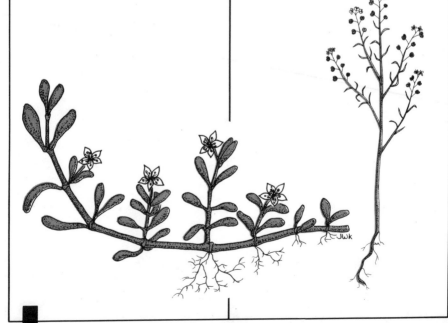

H E R B

HORSEMINT
Monarda punctata

- Mint family: Lamiaceae
- Perennial, stems four-sided, hairy
- Leaves: opposite, elliptic-lanceolate, margins toothed
- Flowers: yellow with purple spots, two-lipped, lavender leafy bracts below flowers, July–Sept.
- Fruits: four tiny nutlets per flower, Sept.–Oct.
- Habitats: dunes, weed in disturbed areas
- Leaves smell of mint

CAPE WEED
Lippia nodiflora

- Verbena family: Verbenaceae
- Perennial, stems upright or flattened on ground, four-sided
- Leaves: opposite, elliptic-obovate, margins toothed
- Flowers: tiny lavender, tubular flowers on leafy heads
- Fruits: nutlets, May–frost
- Habitats: dune swales, weed in sand

GRASS

- Graminoides, or grass-like plants, fall into three distinct families: true grasses, sedges and rushes
- true grass leaves are linear-shaped, often flat or inrolled
- sedge leaves are three-sided
- rush leaves are cylindrical
- true grass and sedge flowers are called spikelets; flat or ovoid florets enclosed by scale-like bracts
- rushes have brownish scale-like flowers

OCEAN DUNE PLANTS

G R A S S

Stems triangular in cross section, does not roll easily between your fingers; spikelets rounded, ovoid, many overlapping scales per spikelet; nutlets are two- or three-sided

Spikelets in terminal compact clusters; five or six white and green showy bracts below spikelets; leaves three-sided at top—WHITE-TOPPED SEDGE *Dichromena colorata* (see page 58)

Spikelets in loose clusters; showy bracts absent; leaves flat or inrolled—MARSH SEDGE *Fimbristylis spadicea* (see page 58)

GRASSES

Spikelet a spiny bur—SANDSPURS *Cenchrus tribuloides* (see page 59)

Spikelets not in t' rows on one side flowering stem

Stems cylindrical in cross section, rolls easily between your fingers; spikelets ovoid, flat, or spiny, few scales per spikelet; grains flat or ovoid

Spikelet not a spiny bur

Spikelets in two rows on one side of flowering stem

Spikes finger-like, radiating from one point; spikelets club-shaped, brownish; stems often creeping or rooting at nodes; leaves basal or low on stems, to 15 cm long, flattened in one plane—FINGER GRASS *Chloris petraea* (see page 59)

Spikes not finger-like; spikelets narrow ascending, purplish; stems upright; leaves overlap along stems, to 60 cm long, inrolled, margins with teeth near tip—SALT MEADOW HAY *Spartina patens* (see page 60)

Spikelets ovoid, hemispheric and hardened, yellow-green—RUNNING BEACH GRASS *Panicum amarum* (see page 61)

Spikelets in solitary racemes; "fuzzy" beard longer than spikelets; leaves and stems purplish or bluish—BLUESTEM *Andropogon scoparius* (see page 61)

Spikelets lanceolate or flattened, not hemispheric and hardened

Spikelets in panicles; "fuzzy" beard absent; leaves and stems not usually purplish or bluish

Spikelets small, less than 1 cm long, not oat-like

Spikelets large, to 3 cm long; flat, yellowish, oat-like, in dense panicles; a dominant plant on dunes generally south of Cape Hatteras—SEA OATS *Uniola paniculata* (see page 60)

Spikelets in dense, spike-like panicles, narrowly cylindric; spikelets without awns, yellowish; a dominant plant on dunes generally north of Cape Hatteras—AMERICAN BEACH GRASS *Ammophila breviligulata* (see page 62)

Spikelets in loose, open panicles; long awns give an "angel-hair" appearance; often purplish—PURPLE MUHLY *Muhlenbergia capillaris* (see page 62)

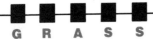

G R A S S

WHITE-TOPPED SEDGE
Dichromena colorata

- Sedge family: Cyperaceae
- Perennial with elongate rhizomes, stems triangular
- Leaves: three-sided
- Flowers: spikelets ovoid, in terminal clusters; scales spiral, overlapping; in terminal clusters; five to six unequal white and green bracts below flowers
- Fruits: yellowish-brown nutlets, triangular, May–Sept.
- Habitats: dune swales, sand-flats, savannahs

MARSH SEDGE
Fimbristylis spadicea

- Sedge family: Cyperaceae
- Perennial with rhizomes, stems triangular
- Leaves: linear, rolled inward
- Flowers: spikelets ovoid, in loose cymes; scales spiral, overlapping
- Fruits: brown nutlets, two-sided, July–Sept.
- Habitats: dune swales, dune meadows, brackish marshes, savannahs

G R A S S

SANDSPUR
Cenchrus tribuloides

- Grass family: Poaceae
- Annual or perennial, stems branching, roots at nodes
- Leaves: linear, glabrous to hairy
- Flowers: spikelets ovoid, in racemes, bracts "bur" densely hairy with long barbed spines
- Fruits: grain covered by green spiny bur, Aug.–Oct.
- Habitats: dunes, weed in sand
- *Cenchrus longispinus:* short spines, non-hairy, weed in disturbed areas
- Unpleasant to walk on barefooted!

FINGER GRASS
Chloris petraea

- Grass family: Poaceae
- Perennial with rhizomes, stems often creeping, roots at nodes
- Leaves: linear, basal and low along stems
- Flowers: spikelets club-shaped, brownish, in two rows on one side of flowering stems, spikes finger-like
- Fruits: grain yellowish, June–Oct.
- Habitats: dunes, sand flats, weedy

G R A S S

SALT MEADOW HAY
Spartina patens

- Grass family: Poaceae
- Perennial with rhizomes, stems cylindrical, hollow
- Leaves: linear, rolled inward or flat, margins with tiny teeth near tip, leaf sheaths overlapping
- Flowers: spikelets lanceolate, purplish, in ascending spikes, often in two rows on one side of flowering stems, June–Sept.
- Fruits: grains olive-colored
- Habitats: dune swales, dune meadows, salt marsh edges
- Used for livestock grazing
- Salt marsh cord grass, *Spartina alterniflora:* broader leaves, more robust, in salt marshes

SEA OATS
Uniola paniculata

- Grass family: Poaceae
- Perennial with rhizomes
- Leaves: linear, rolled inward, basal and along stem
- Flowers: flat, yellowish oat-like spikelets, to 3 cm long, in dense panicles, June–Nov.
- Fruits: grain, propagates mainly by rhizomes
- Habitat: dunes
- Vital to dune stabilization

■ ■ ■ ■ ■
G   R   A   S   S

RUNNING BEACH GRASS
Panicum amarum

- Grass family: Poaceae
- Perennial with elongate rhizomes, roots at lower nodes
- Leaves: linear, whitish-green, upper leaf may extend above spikelets
- Flowers: spikelets ovoid, yellowish, in narrow panicles
- Fruits: purplish grain, Oct.
- Habitat: dunes
- Silver bunch grass, *Panicum amarulum:* tufted, short rhizomes, in marshes and sandflats, rare

BLUESTEM
Andropogon scoparius

- Grass family: Poaceae
- Perennial with rhizomes, stems purplish
- Leaves: linear, purplish, hairy, rolled inward
- Flowers: spikelets lanceolate, yellowish, in solitary racemes, bearded "fuzzy appearance," long twisted hairs called awns
- Fruits: grain purplish or yellowish, Aug.–Oct.
- Habitats: dunes, weed in disturbed areas
- Broom sedge, *Andropogon virginicus:* racemes usually two, bearded, very "fuzzy appearance" straight awns, in marshes and bogs

OCEAN DUNE PLANTS

G R A S S

AMERICAN BEACH GRASS
Ammophila breviligulata

- Grass family: Poaceae
- Perennial with rhizomes
- Leaves: linear, rolled inward
- Flowers: yellowish lanceolate spikelets, in dense spike-like panicles, Aug.–Sept.
- Fruits: grain
- Habitat: dunes, infrequent
- Planted to bind sand on ocean-front property

PURPLE MUHLY
Muhlenbergia capillaris

- Grass family: Poaceae
- Perennial, grows in clumps
- Leaves: linear, flat or rolled inward
- Flowers: spikelets lanceolate, purplish, long hairs called awns, in loose panicles, delicate "angel-hair" appearance
- Fruits: purplish grain, Sept.–Oct.
- Habitats: dunes, dry woods, savannahs

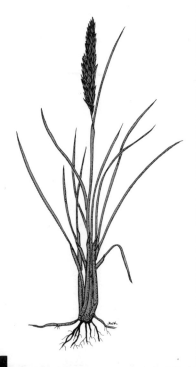

Other plants may occur on dunes or may look similar to the species illustrated. It is possible to find a number of roadside weeds that frequently colonize dunes once disturbed by ocean-front development. Note that many dune and weedy plants also colonize dredge spoil islands located along coastal waterways. Many of these plants are listed here.

TREES
Juniperus silicicola—Southern red cedar: see *Juniperus virginiana*
Quercus laurifolia—laurel oak: see *Quercus virginiana*

SHRUBS
Baccharis glomeruliflora groundsel-tree: see *Baccharis halimifolia*
Daubentonia punicea—rattle-box (Fabaceae)
Leaves pinnately compound, flowers reddish-orange in racemes, legume winged, seeds rattle when dry. June–Nov., weedy
Iva frutescens—marsh elder: see *Iva imbricata*
Myrica pensylvanica—bayberry: see *Myrica cerifera*
Opuntia compressa—prickly pear: see *Opuntia drummondii*
Yucca gloriosa—Spanish bayonet: see *Yucca aloifolia*

VINES
Calystegia soldanella—beach morning glory: see *Ipomoea sagittata*
Ipomoea stolonifera—creeping morning glory: see *Ipomoea sagittata*
Melothria pendula—creeping cucumber (Cucurbitaceae)
Tendrils, leaves palmately lobed, flowers yellow, tubular-shape, cucumber-like fruit. June–frost, dunes, thickets, mashes, weedy
Passiflora lutea—yellow passion flower (Passifloraceae)
Tendrils, leaves palmately lobed, mottled, flowers yellowish-green, black berry. June–Oct. dunes, thickets, woodlands

HERBS
Achillea millefolium—yarrow (Asteraceae)
Leaves pinnately dissected, flowering heads off-white or pink, flat-topped, nutlets. April–frost, weedy
Ambrosia artemisiifolia—ragweed (Asteraceae)
Leaves pinnately dissected, green heads in racemes, beaked nutlets. Aug.–frost, weedy

CONTINUED

ADDITIONAL PLANTS

Arenaria lanuginosa—sandwort (Caryophyllaceae) Delicate plant, stems trailing, leaves opposite, elliptic to oblanceolate, flowers in axils, petals absent, capsules. May–July, infrequent on dunes

Argemone mexicana—prickly poppy (Papaveraceae) Leaves spiny, clasping to stem, bright yellow sap, flowers bright yellow, spiny capsules. April–May, weedy, rare

Asparagus officinalis—asparagus (Liliaceae) Leaves filiform to linear, flowers white, tiny bell-shape, red berry, shoots edible. April–Oct., weedy

Atriplex arenaria—seabeach orach: see *Atriplex patula*

Bidens bipinnata—Spanish needles (Asteraceae) Leaves pinnately dissected, flowers in heads, yellow ray flowers present or absent, nutlets. July–Oct., weedy

Cakile edentula—sea rocket: see *Cakile harperi*

Chenopodium ambrosioides—Mexican tea (Chenopodiaceae) Leaves lanceolate to elliptic, dentate margins, aromatic, inflorescence leafy, flowers and fruits inconspicuous. July–frost, weedy

Cnidoscolus stimulosus—sand nettle (Euphorbiaceae) Leaves palmately lobed, dentate, stinging hairs, flowers white, tubular, capsule. March–Aug., dry pine-oak woods, weedy

Commelina erecta—day flower (Commelinaceae) Leaves lanceolate to elliptic, flowers with two blue petals, in leafy spathes, capsule. June–Oct., weedy

Diodia teres—diodia (Rubiaceae) Leaves opposite, linear to lanceolate, flowers white, tubular, four petals, leathery fruit. June–frost, weedy

Eupatorium capillifolium—dog fennel (Asteraceae) Leaves bipinnately dissected to filiform, cream-colored heads in open panicles, nutlets. Sept.–frost, weedy

Euphorbia ammannioides—dune spurge: see *Euphorbia polygonifolia*

Gnaphalium obtusifolium—rabbit tobacco, cudweed (Asteraceae) White woolly stems, papery white heads, nutlets. Aug.–Oct., weedy

Hydrocotyle umbellata—marsh pennywort: see *Hydrocotyle bonariensis*

Iresine rhizomatosa—dune amaranth: see *Amaranthus pumilus*

Krigia virginica—dwarf dandelion (Asteraceae) Leaves elliptic to oblanceolate, dentate to deeply cut, yellow ray flowers, like a small dandelion, nutlets with pappus hairs. March–June, weedy

Oenothera laciniata—evening primrose: see *Oenothera humifusa*

Rumex acetosella—sheepsorrel, sour-grass (Polygonaceae) Stems with swollen nodes, stipule leaves, leaves with basal lobes, flowering racemes green, pink, red or purple, petals absent, nutlets. March–July, weedy

Salsola kali—Russian thistle (Chenopodiaceae) Leaves fleshy, spiny, flowers inconspicuous, plants pink in autumn. June–frost, weedy, rare

Sesuvium maritimum—sea purslane: see *Sesuvium portulascastrum*

Solanum gracile—nightshade: dunes, marshes, see *Physalis viscosa* ssp. *maritima*

Sonchus asper—sow thistle: see *Lactuca canadensis*

Xanthium strumarium—cocklebur (Asteraceae) Leaves triangular-ovate, lobed, margins serrate, base heart-shaped, fruit bur-like, spiny. July–frost, beaches, weedy

GRASSES

Andropogon virginicus—broom sedge: see *Andropogon scoparius*

Cenchrus longispinus—sandspur: see *Cenchrus tribuloides*

Panicum amarulum—silver bunch grass: see *Panicum amarum*

Spartina alterniflora—salt marsh cord grass: see *Spartina patens*

INDEX OF
SCIENTIFIC NAMES

INDEX OF COMMON NAMES

REFERENCES

Au, Shu-Fun. 1974. *Vegetation and Ecological Processes on Shackleford Banks, North Carolina.* National Park Service Scientific Monograph Series. No. 6. U.S. Government Printing Office.

Boyce, Steven. 1954. "The Salt Spray Community." *Ecological Monographs* 20:29–68.

Brown, Clair A. 1959. *The Vegetation of the Outer Banks of North Carolina.* Louisiana State University Press. Baton Rouge, LA.

Clark, John (Ed.). 1976. *Barrier Islands and Beaches.* Technical Proceedings of the 1976 Barrier Islands workshop. Annapolis, MD.

Dunes of Dare Garden Club. 1980. *Wildflowers of the Outer Banks, Kitty Hawk to Hatteras.* UNC Press, Chapel Hill.

Evans, Jonathon. Nov. 1985. "North Carolina Barrier Island Flora." Computer file at Duke University Marine Laboratory, unpublished.

Gleasner, Diana and Bill Gleasner. 1980. *Sea Islands of the South.* The East Woods Press.

Godfrey, Paul J. and Melinda M. Godfrey. 1976. *Barrier Island Ecology of Cape Lookout National Seashore and Vicinity, North Carolina.* National Park Service Scientific Monograph Series. No. 9. U.S. Government Printing Office.

Graetz, Karl E. 1973. *Seacoast Plants of the Carolinas for Conservation and Beautification.* UNC Sea Grant publication UNC-SG-73-06.

Leatherman, Stephen. 1982. *Barrier Island Handbook.* University of Maryland Press.

Pilkey, Orrin H. Jr., William J. Neal, Orrin H. Pilkey Sr. and Stanley R. Riggs. 1978. *From Currituck to Calabash, Living with North Carolina's Barrier Islands.* Duke University Press.

Radford, Albert E., Harry E. Ahles and C. R. Bell. 1968. *Manual of the Vascular Flora of the Carolinas.* UNC Press, Chapel Hill.

Spitsbergen, Judith M. 1980. *Seacoast Life, An Ecological Guide to Natural Seashore Communities in North Carolina.* UNC Press, Chapel Hill.

Wilson, Elizabeth Jean (Kraus). June 1981. *A Guide to Salt Marsh Plants Common to North Carolina.* UNC Sea Grant publication UNC-SG-81-04.

The author wishes to recognize the following people who aided in the completion of all phases of this book.

To the UNC Sea Grant Program for publishing the book, and to Sarah Friday and Lundie Spence for editing and scientific review of the manuscript.
To Charles McNeill, director of the North Carolina Maritime Museum, and the staff, for support of this project. To Rosalie Piner and JoAnne Powell, museum staff, for reading and reviewing the manuscript.
To Carolyn Hoss, John Fussell, William Blankley and Kathryn Blankley for collecting and donating herbarium specimens used for drawings.
To Brian Kraus, husband and artist, for critique of drawings, and overall encouragement.

■
NOTES